TEAM SPIRIT ®

SMART BOOKS FOR YOUNG FANS

THE TORONTO BLUE JAYS

BY
MARK STEWART

NORWOODHOUSE PRESS
CHICAGO, ILLINOIS

Norwood House Press
P.O. Box 316598
Chicago, Illinois 60631

For information regarding Norwood House Press, please visit our website at:
www.norwoodhousepress.com or call 866-565-2900.

All photos courtesy of Getty Images except the following:
Black Book Partners Archives (9, 10, 16, 17, 22, 33, 38, 42 top left, 43 bottom left & right),
Tom DiPace (10, 11), Associated Press (14),
Topps, Inc. (15, 21, 28, 30, 31, 34 all, 35 top left & right, 39, 40, 43 top right, 45),
O-Pee-Chee, Ltd. (26, 41), Matt Richman (48).
Cover Photo: Scott Halleran/Getty Images

The memorabilia and artifacts pictured in this book are presented for educational and informational purposes,
and come from the collection of the author.

Editor: Mike Kennedy
Designer: Ron Jaffe
Project Management: Black Book Partners, LLC.
Special thanks to Topps, Inc.

Library of Congress Cataloging-in-Publication Data

Stewart, Mark, 1960-
  The Toronto Blue Jays / by Mark Stewart. -- Library ed.
      p. cm. -- (Team spirit)
  Includes bibliographical references and index.
  Summary: "A Team Spirit Baseball edition featuring the Toronto Blue Jays
that chronicles the history and accomplishments of the team. Includes access
to the Team Spirit website, which provides additional information, updates
and photos"--Provided by publisher.
  ISBN 978-1-59953-500-5 (library : alk. paper) -- ISBN 978-1-60357-380-1
(ebook) 1. Toronto Blue Jays (Baseball team)--History--Juvenile
literature. I. Title.
  GV875.T67S66 2012
  796.357'6409713541--dc23
                                              2011048201

Manufactured in the United States of America in North Mankato, Minnesota.
196N—012012

COVER PHOTO: The Blue Jays celebrate a victory in 2011.

TABLE OF CONTENTS

CHAPTER	PAGE
MEET THE BLUE JAYS	4
GLORY DAYS	6
HOME TURF	12
DRESSED FOR SUCCESS	14
WE WON!	16
GO-TO GUYS	20
CALLING THE SHOTS	24
ONE GREAT DAY	26
LEGEND HAS IT	28
IT REALLY HAPPENED	30
TEAM SPIRIT	32
TIMELINE	34
FUN FACTS	36
TALKING BASEBALL	38
GREAT DEBATES	40
FOR THE RECORD	42
PINPOINTS	44
GLOSSARY	46
EXTRA INNINGS	47
INDEX	48

ABOUT OUR GLOSSARY

In this book, there may be several words that you are reading for the first time. Some are sports words, some are new vocabulary words, and some are familiar words that are used in an unusual way. All of these words are defined on page 46. Throughout the book, sports words appear in **bold type**. Regular vocabulary words appear in ***bold italic type***.

MEET THE BLUE JAYS

The blue jay is a fearless animal that will drive others away from its territory. Jays take on all invaders, including birds many times their size. They are also smart and *resourceful*. Baseball lovers say the same things about the Toronto Blue Jays. In fact, it might be the perfect name for the team.

The Blue Jays are the only Canadian club in the big leagues. The entire country roots for them. Almost all of the players on the team come from places outside Canada. But they still play as if they were born there. Many Jays make their homes in Canada during the season. They proudly sing the country's national anthem before each game.

This book tells the story of the Blue Jays. They play with great pride and *passion*. They do not back down, no matter how strong their opponent is. And they put winning players on the field every year.

Yunel Escobar does not let a sliding runner stop him from throwing to first. The Jays are always on the lookout for tough and talented players like him.

5

GLORY DAYS

Baseball has been played in Canada nearly as long as it has in the United States. Yet it was not until the 1960s that **Major League Baseball** placed teams north of the U.S. border. In 1977, the Blue Jays joined the **American League (AL)**. They became the second Canadian club in the big leagues. The Montreal Expos started play before them, in the **National League (NL)**. Ever since the Expos moved to Washington D.C. and became the Nationals in 2005, the Blue Jays have been Canada's only team.

Like all new teams, the Blue Jays had to start with unwanted players from other clubs. They also found unknown young players and gave them their first chance. Toronto's top stars in those early days included Bob Bailor, John Mayberry, Ron Fairly, Roy Howell, Rick Cerone,

and Alfredo Griffin. Unfortunately, the Blue Jays struggled to win—the team finished last in the **AL East** five years in a row.

Toronto fans were patient with their Blue Jays. The team spent a lot of time and money getting young players ready for the major leagues. In the 1980s, those players made Toronto one of the best teams in baseball. Infielders Willie Upshaw, Fred McGriff, and Tony Fernandez combined with outfielders George Bell, Lloyd Moseby, and Jesse Barfield to provide powerful hitting. Dave Stieb and Jimmy Key led a good pitching staff. Toronto won the AL East in 1985.

In 1989, the Blue Jays moved into a magnificent new ballpark called SkyDome. Millions of fans came to visit the stadium. The team used the money it made from ticket sales to improve its lineup. In 1992 and 1993, the Blue Jays won back-to-back **World Series** championships. Those teams were a perfect blend of young stars

and reliable **veterans**. John Olerud, Roberto Alomar, Devon White, David Wells, David Cone, and Pat Hentgen were just reaching their best years. Jack Morris, Dave Stewart, Joe Carter, Dave Winfield, and Paul Molitor took advantage of their last chance at glory.

Later in the 1990s, the Blue Jays looked like they were ready to capture another championship, but the team came up short. Toronto still gave fans plenty to cheer about. Carlos Delgado, Shawn Green, and Shannon Stewart were three of the best hitters in the league. Roger

Clemens pitched two years for Toronto and led the AL in victories, strikeouts, and **earned run average (ERA)** each season. He also won the **Cy Young Award** twice.

LEFT: Dave Stieb fires a fastball. He was the team's top pitcher in the 1980s.
ABOVE: Joe Carter was one of many experienced Toronto stars of the 1990s.

9

As the 21st century began, the Blue Jays kept trying to repeat their championship formula. Many talented players wore the Toronto uniform during this time, including Vernon Wells, Ted Lilly, A.J. Burnett, Brett Cecil, and Roy Halladay. Of these stars, no one was better than Halladay. He was an **All-Star** six times and won the Cy Young Award in 2003. Despite Halladay's great pitching, Toronto did not return to the World Series.

The Blue Jays took a big step in rebuilding their team when they traded for Jose Bautista in 2008. Toronto surrounded him with a solid core of players, including Yunel Escobar, Adam Lind, J.P. Arencibia,

ABOVE: Roy Halladay   **RIGHT**: Jose Bautista

and Ricky Romero. Bautista added great power to the lineup. He led the league in home runs in 2010 and 2011.

The Blue Jays know what it takes to get to the World Series. Each spring, they leave training camp with a group of players they believe can help them win the **pennant**. If the Jays have made good decisions and the players do their best, there may be another championship banner flying over Toronto one day soon.

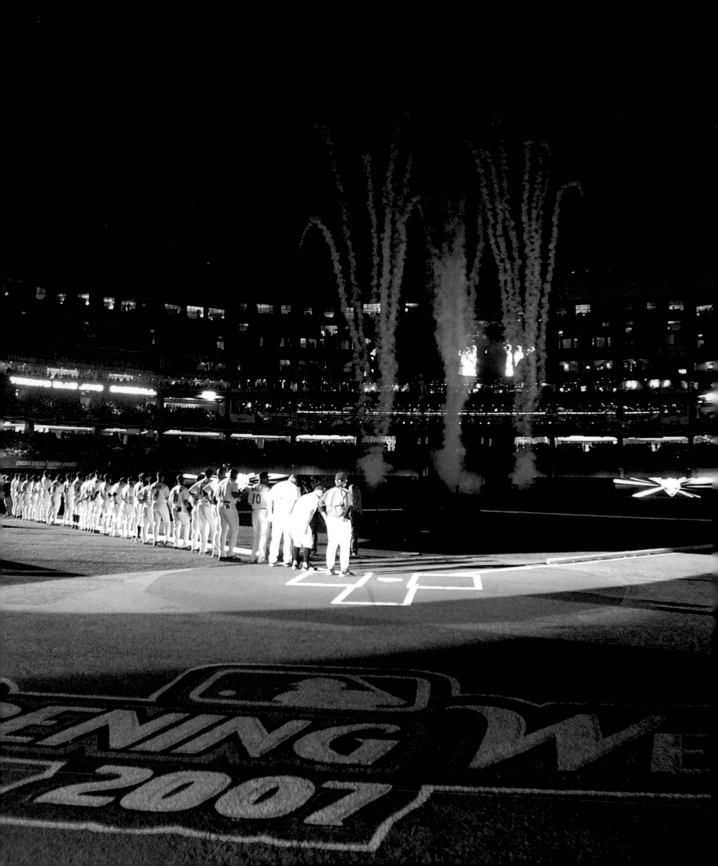

HOME TURF

The first home for the Blue Jays was Exhibition Stadium. It was built for the Argonauts of the *Canadian Football League (CFL)*. Because of the size of a CFL field, the stadium had some seats for baseball games that were very far from home plate. A few were more than 800 feet (244 meters) away!

In 1989, the Blue Jays moved into SkyDome. It was the first stadium with a *retractable* roof. The team closes the roof to protect the fans from cold and rainy weather. The stadium also has a 340-room hotel attached to it. Seventy rooms have views of the field. The Blue Jays still play in this park. In 2005, it was renamed the Rogers Centre after the team's new owner, Rogers Communications—a large telephone and Internet company in Canada.

BY THE NUMBERS

- The Blue Jays' stadium has 49,260 seats.
- The distance from home plate to the left field foul pole is 328 feet (100 meters).
- The distance from home plate to the center field fence is 400 feet (122 meters).
- The distance from home plate to the right field foul pole is 328 feet (100 meters).

The hotel rooms that overlook the field can be seen in this photo of the Blue Jays' stadium.

DRESSED FOR SUCCESS

Light blue, dark blue, black, and white are the colors of a blue jay. They have also been Toronto's colors since the team began in 1977. Red—the national color of Canada—is also used. For a while, the team featured less blue and more black and silver in its uniform. For the 2012 season, Toronto went back to blue and returned to a *futuristic* lettering style like they used in their early years.

STEVE STAGGS

The company that first owned the Blue Jays hoped that fans would call the club the "Blues." But everyone called them the "Jays." Before their 2012 uniform change, that was what their home uniform said across the front. They also used the letter *T* on their caps for several seasons. Now the caps will look more like they did during Toronto's championship years.

The team's *logo* has always featured a blue jay. It also includes a small red maple leaf, which is very important to the people of Canada. The maple leaf is a symbol of national pride.

LEFT: Adam Lind models the team's new uniform for the 2012 season.
ABOVE: The team's 2012 uniforms look more like the one Steve Staggs is wearing on his 1970s trading card.

WE WON!

There is nothing easy about winning the World Series. But what's even harder is winning a championship two years in a row. That's because other teams love to beat the current champions. In recent years, only two teams have won back-to-back World

Series. One of those teams was the Blue Jays. They were champions in 1992 and 1993.

The players who made the Blue Jays go in the 1990s were Devon White and Roberto Alomar. They stole bases, scored runs, and played great defense. The team's power hitters were Joe Carter and John Olerud. In 1992, the Blue Jays got a terrific year from 40-year-old Dave Winfield. In 1993, they added three other veterans—Rickey Henderson, Tony Fernandez, and Paul Molitor.

Toronto's pitching was also first-rate. In 1992, the starters included Jack Morris, David Cone, and Juan Guzman. The team's best relief pitcher was Tom Henke. In 1993, Pat Hentgen was the leader of the pitching staff. He combined with Guzman, Jimmy Key, and Dave Stewart to give Toronto a great **starting rotation**. Duane Ward was the star of the **bullpen**.

The Blue Jays faced the Atlanta Braves in the 1992 World Series. The first four games were close and exciting. Toronto won three of them—two with thrilling finishes in the ninth inning. The hitting heroes in those victories were Ed Sprague and Candy Maldonado. Neither player was a star, but both came up big when the pressure was on.

After the Braves won Game 5 to keep things close, Toronto responded with a victory in Game 6 to capture the championship. Winfield, in his 20th year in the majors, finally earned a World Series ring. It was his double in the 11th inning that delivered the 4–3 win for the Blue Jays. The **Most Valuable Player (MVP)** of the series was catcher Pat Borders. He hit .450 and called good games for the Toronto pitchers.

In 1993, the Blue Jays faced the Philadelphia Phillies in a World Series that featured a lot of hitting. Toronto won two of the first three games by scores of 8–5 and 10–3. In Game 4, the Phillies were leading 14–9 after seven innings. It looked as if they would tie the series—until Toronto scored six runs in the eighth inning to win 15–14! The Blue Jays took a commanding lead in the series.

The Phillies would not give up. They won the next night 2–0 in a pitching duel between Guzman and Curt Schilling. The Phillies also played well in Game 6. They led Toronto 6–5 going into the bottom of the ninth inning. Henderson and Molitor got on base against Mitch Williams. Carter then stepped up to the plate and smashed a home run into the left field seats. The Blue Jays won 8–6 and celebrated their second championship.

LEFT: Pat Borders gets a hit during the 1992 World Series.
ABOVE: Joe Carter celebrates his home run in 1993.

GO-TO GUYS

To be a true star in baseball, you need more than a quick bat and a strong arm. You have to be a "go-to guy"—someone the manager wants on the pitcher's mound or in the batter's box when it matters most. Fans of the Blue Jays have had a lot to cheer about over the years, including these great stars ...

 ## THE PIONEERS

DAVE STIEB   Pitcher

• BORN: 7/22/1957   • PLAYED FOR TEAM: 1979 TO 1992 & 1998

Dave Stieb was famous for his great curveball and his fighting spirit on the pitcher's mound. He was picked to play in the All-Star Game seven times. Stieb was one of the most popular Blue Jays ever.

GEORGE BELL   Outfielder

• BORN: 10/21/1959   • PLAYED FOR TEAM: 1981 TO 1990

George Bell, Lloyd Moseby, and Jesse Barfield made up Toronto's great outfield of the 1980s. Bell was the best of the three. In 1987, he hit 47 home runs and became the first player from the Dominican Republic to be named the AL MVP.

TONY FERNANDEZ   Shortstop

- BORN: 6/30/1962
- PLAYED FOR TEAM: 1983 TO 1990, 1993,
  1998 TO 1999, & 2001

Tony Fernandez was a smooth-fielding shortstop who also got a lot of important hits for Toronto. In the 1993 World Series, he set a record for shortstops by driving in nine runs.

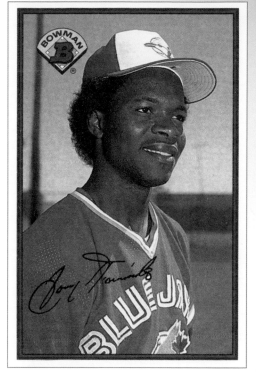

JIMMY KEY   Pitcher

- BORN: 4/22/1961
- PLAYED FOR TEAM: 1984 TO 1992

Jimmy Key was a master at throwing off the timing of batters. He could deliver several different pitches at different speeds and hit any target the catcher gave him. Key won 116 games in nine seasons for the Blue Jays.

TOM HENKE   Pitcher

- BORN: 12/21/1957   • PLAYED FOR TEAM: 1985 TO 1992

Tom Henke's nickname was the "Terminator." When he came into a game, the other team usually did not stand a chance. Henke had a blazing fastball and another pitch that dipped down as it neared home plate.

ABOVE: Tony Fernandez

JOE CARTER   Outfielder

- BORN: 3/7/1960   • PLAYED FOR TEAM: 1991 TO 1997

Joe Carter was one of baseball's best hitters under pressure. He loved to bat with runners on base. His home run to win the 1993 World Series was one of the great moments in team history.

ROBERTO ALOMAR   Second Baseman

- BORN: 2/5/1968

- PLAYED FOR TEAM: 1991 TO 1995

Roberto Alomar was one of the finest all-around players in baseball during the 1990s. He was at his best during his years in Toronto. Alomar was an All-Star and won a **Gold Glove** in each of his five seasons with the Blue Jays.

CARLOS DELGADO   First Baseman

- BORN: 6/25/1972

- PLAYED FOR TEAM: 1993 TO 2004

Carlos Delgado was one of the most powerful hitters ever to wear a Toronto uniform. In 2003, he became just the fifth player in AL history to slug four home runs in a game.

ROY HALLADAY — Pitcher

- BORN: 5/14/1977
- PLAYED FOR TEAM: 1998 TO 2009

Roy Halladay threw very hard when he joined the Blue Jays, but he pitched too high in the strike zone. The team sent him back to the **minors** to learn better control. Halladay returned as one of the best pitchers in baseball. He won the Cy Young Award in 2003.

VERNON WELLS — Outfielder

- BORN: 12/8/1978
- PLAYED FOR TEAM: 1999 TO 2010

Vernon Wells was a substitute to start his career with the Blue Jays. After a few seasons, he developed into a star. Wells hit, played defense, and ran the bases as well as anyone in the AL. In 2003, he led the league with 215 hits.

JOSE BAUTISTA — Outfielder

- BORN: 10/19/1980   • FIRST YEAR WITH TEAM: 2008

Four different teams gave up on Jose Bautista before he joined the Blue Jays. In Toronto, he changed his swing to increase his power. The fans there were glad he did. Bautista led the AL with 54 homers in 2010 and 43 in 2011.

LEFT: Roberto Alomar
ABOVE: Vernon Wells

CALLING THE SHOTS

When the Blue Jays hire a manager, they can be very picky. They look for leaders who have a deep knowledge of baseball. But the Jays also like managers who understand how to get the most out of different players with different skills and personalities. This sounds easier than it is.

Over the years, Toronto has been able to find several managers who fit the team's needs. In the early 1980s, Bobby Cox made his young club believe it was as good as any team in the AL East. The Blue Jays had their first winning season in 1983, and they barely missed their first trip to the World Series in 1985.

Seven years later, the Jays faced off against Cox in the World Series when he was the manager of the Atlanta Braves. Cito Gaston was now the leader in the Toronto dugout. He had been one of Cox's coaches with the Blue Jays. They had a fun time trying to out-guess each other—each knew everything the other wanted to do! Gaston got the best of Cox, and the Jays won in six games.

Gaston was very popular with the Blue Jays. The players respected his knowledge and leadership. They were also aware that he had

Cito Gaston led the Blue Jays to championships in 1992 and 1993.

been a very good player. In fact, Gaston was an All-Star for the San Diego Padres in the 1970s. What people remember most about him as a player is how carefully he listened to instruction and coaching. He expected the same of his own players in Toronto.

Gaston managed the Blue Jays from 1989 to 1997. During that time, they went to the **playoffs** four times and won the World Series twice. In 2008, after many years in the team's business office, Gaston returned to the Toronto dugout. The Jays were playing poorly and had sunk to last place. They went on a 10-game winning streak in his first season and finished with a record of 86–76.

ONE GREAT DAY

The 1987 season was a good one for fans who liked to see home runs. All year long, batters knocked balls out of the park at a record pace. The most amazing game that season took place in

Toronto Blue Jays
outfield LLOYD MOSEBY voltigeur
Card Number 24 of 24 - Carte Numéro 24 de 24
© 1981 O-Pee-Chee Co. Ltd. Printed in Canada - Imprimé au Canada

September in Toronto between the Blue Jays and Baltimore Orioles. The Jays were fighting the Detroit Tigers for the AL East lead. Every victory was precious.

In the second inning, Ernie Whitt—one of Toronto's most popular players—hit a home run against Ken Dixon of the Orioles. Before the young pitcher knew it, Rance Mulliniks and Lloyd Moseby each hit two-run homers.

Things got even worse for the Orioles after that as Toronto's hitters went homer-crazy. Mulliniks hit his second of the game, George Bell smashed a pair

LEFT: Lloyd Moseby was one of six Blue Jays to homer against the Baltimore Orioles.
RIGHT: Fred McGriff connects for a home run.

of home runs, and Whitt hit another long bomb.

In the seventh inning, Rob Ducey blasted a ball into the seats for the team's eighth home run. Whitt then hit his third home run of the game. The final blow came off the bat of Fred McGriff in the eighth inning.

Toronto won the game 18–3. The 10 home runs hit by the Blue Jays set a record for a major-league game. Afterwards, a reporter asked Mike Boddicker of the Orioles about the historic power display. "We tried looking for the record-breaking ball out beyond the fence in right," said the pitcher, "but there were too many of them bunched up there!"

LEGEND HAS IT

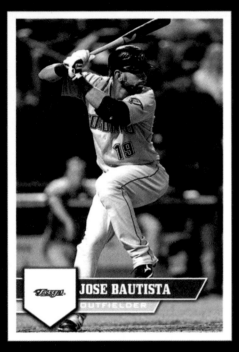

WHICH BLUE JAYS SLUGGER WAITED MORE THAN TWO YEARS BEFORE HITTING HIS FIRST HOME RUN?

LEGEND HAS IT that Jose Bautista did. Toronto fans are very familiar with the Jose Bautista who blasted 97 homers in 2010 and 2011. They might not recognize the skinny infielder who tried to break into the majors in 2004. That season, Bautista actually played for four teams. He finished the year with the Pittsburgh Pirates. It was not until May of the 2006 season that Bautista finally hit his first home run as a big leaguer.

ABOVE: This sticker shows Jose Bautista in a Toronto uniform. He played for four other teams before he became a Blue Jay.

WHO HAD BASEBALL'S BEST PICK-OFF MOVE IN THE 1970S?

LEGEND HAS IT that Jerry Garvin did. Garvin was one of the original Blue Jays. He was not a great pitcher—many runners reached base against him. Once they were on, however, Garvin was very tough. He threw left-handed, and most runners could not tell until it was too late whether he was going to throw to the catcher or to the first baseman. During the 1977 season, Garvin caught 22 runners leading too far off first base.

WHICH BLUE JAY SUFFERED FROM ARACHNOPHOBIA?

LEGEND HAS IT that Glenallen Hill did. Arachnophobia is a fear of spiders. Hill was a slugger who played for Toronto from 1989 to 1991. He was not afraid of anything, except little eight-legged creatures. One night, Hill had a dream that spiders were chasing him. He jumped out of bed and ran through his apartment in terror. He fell, injured himself, and missed more than two weeks of action.

IT REALLY HAPPENED

L osing is no fun, especially when your team is getting destroyed. That is why many youth leagues have a 10-run "Mercy Rule." After a certain number of innings, if one team is ahead by 10 runs (or more), the umpire ends the game. Of course, there is no Mercy Rule in the big leagues.

That was fine with the fans at Boston's Fenway Park on June 4, 1989. They were having a great time watching their team beat up on Toronto pitching. The Red Sox scored five runs in the first inning, and five more after that. When the Blue Jays came to bat in the seventh inning, the scoreboard told the sad story: Boston 10 Toronto 0.

The crowd barely noticed when the Red Sox walked the first three Blue Jays that inning. When the next batter hit into a double-play, the fans were disappointed that there wouldn't be a shutout. Lloyd Moseby

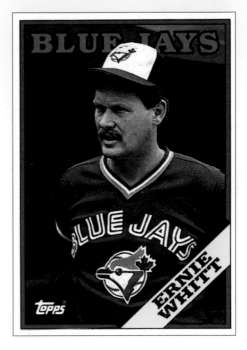

scored from third base on the play. Even so, the Boston crowd wasn't too worried. When Ernie Whitt scored a second run on a double, it still was not a matter of great concern.

Things started to get interesting in the eighth inning. Moseby singled in two runs, and the Blue Jays scored twice more to make the score 10–6. Suddenly, the fans got nervous. The Blue Jays were on a roll. They cut the score to 10–7 with three straight hits in the ninth. Then Whitt hit a screaming line drive into the seats for a **grand slam**. Toronto had the lead!

With the Boston fans now on their feet, the Red Sox were able to tie the game in the bottom of the ninth inning. But there was no stopping the Jays. In the 12th inning, a **rookie** named Junior Felix hit a long home run with a man on base to give Toronto a 13–11 victory. The very next day, the team received a long, loud ovation from their own fans. The heroes had returned from Boston for the first game in SkyDome, their new stadium.

TEAM SPIRIT

Blue Jays fans are not afraid to look a little strange or silly if it means showing a little team spirit. They paint their faces blue, black, and white. They find unusual hats and shirts in team colors. They bring clever signs and banners to the ballpark. Many fans wear the jerseys of the team's great players. Others wear the jerseys of the not-so-great Blue Jays, hoping to bring back memories of the teams from the 1970s.

One of the ways the Blue Jays say *thank you* to their fans is by making sure their ballpark is green. That means they conserve energy and recycle everything they can. Going green is important to the people of Canada and their government. The Jays pitch in by reducing the amount of paper they use, and by buying products made of materials that have already been recycled.

LEFT: A Blue Jays fan proudly wears a blue and white balloon hat.
ABOVE: Vernon Wells signs autographs for fans.

TIMELINE

Tony
Fernandez

1985
The Blue Jays win the
AL East for the first time.

1986
Jesse Barfield and Tony Fernandez become
the first Blue Jays to win Gold Gloves.

1977
The Blue Jays play
their first season.

1988
George Bell hits three
homers on Opening Day.

1992
The Blue Jays become
the first Canadian team
to win the World Series.

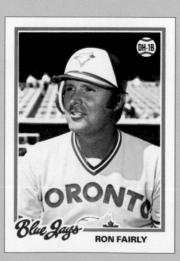

RON FAIRLY

Ron Fairly led
the 1977 Blue Jays
with 19 homers.

Juan Guzman
won 30 games
for the team in
1992 and 1993.

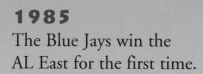

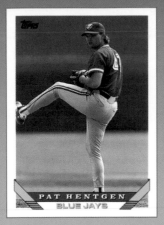

Pat Hentgen went
19–9 in 1993.

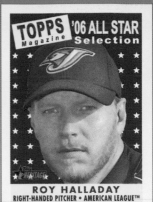

Roy
Halladay

1993
The Blue Jays win
their second World
Series in a row.

2003
Roy Halladay
wins the Cy
Young Award.

2007
Frank Thomas joins
Toronto and slugs
his 500th home run.

1999
Carlos Delgado hits eight
home runs in six games.

2011
Jose Bautista leads the AL in
homers for the second year in a row.

Carlos
Delgado

Fun Facts

What Else You Got?

J.P. Arencibia faced All-Star James Shields of the Tampa Bay Rays in his first big-league at-bat. Arencibia blasted the first pitch he saw for a home run. He hit a second home run later in the game.

Where Do I Play, Coach?

When the Blue Jays drafted John Olerud in 1989, he wasn't sure if they wanted him as a hitter or a pitcher—in college he had been great at both. Toronto made the right decision. Olerud won the batting championship in 1993.

Power Surge

In Toronto's first game, Doug Ault hit home runs in his first two trips to the plate. He hit only nine more the rest of the year.

CHANGE OF SCENERY

On May 28, 1989, George Bell hit a homer in the last game played in Exhibition Stadium. A few days later, he homered in the first game in SkyDome.

CUTTING IT CLOSE

In the 1992 World Series, the Blue Jays got each of their four wins by a single run.

LUCKY SEVEN

Jose Bautista wore six different numbers for five different teams before settling on number 19 with the Blue Jays in 2010.

BLESS YOU

Blue Jays pitcher Ricky Romero was off to one of the fastest starts in team history in 2009—and then suffered one of the weirdest injuries. Romero sneezed so hard one day that he strained a muscle and had to go on the **disabled list**.

LEFT: John Olerud
ABOVE: George Bell

TALKING BASEBALL

"Toronto will forever have a special place in my heart. The memories will last a lifetime and so will my gratitude."

► ROY HALLADAY, ON HIS LOVE OF BLUE JAYS FANS

"1993 in Toronto was probably my number-one memory, because it was the only time I was able to enter baseball's winner's circle."

► PAUL MOLITOR, ON TORONTO'S SECOND CHAMPIONSHIP

"If you can't smile and have fun, you're in trouble."

► CARLOS DELGADO, ON ENJOYING LIFE AS A BIG-LEAGUER

"I dreamed of that moment when I was a little kid. I'd be sitting at my father's garage and daydreaming about that moment. I even wrote it down a few times: 'My dream is to hit a home run to win the World Series.'"

▶ **JOE CARTER**, ON HIS HOME RUN THAT WON THE 1993 WORLD SERIES

"Hitting is just *repetition*. The more you hit, the better you're going to get."

▶ **VERNON WELLS**, ON THE IMPORTANCE OF PRACTICE

"When I grew up, people would tell me, 'You'll never make it to the big leagues.' But when I talk to kids, I tell them everything is possible and to never let anybody say you can't do it."

▶ **RICKY ROMERO**, ON FOLLOWING YOUR DREAMS

"It's just a matter of having an opportunity to show what I can do. I'm getting that now."

▶ **JOSE BAUTISTA**, ON LETTING HIS TALENT SHINE THROUGH WITH THE JAYS

LEFT: Carlos Delgado
RIGHT: Ricky Romero

GREAT DEBATES

People who root for the Blue Jays love to compare their favorite moments, teams, and players. Some debates have been going on for years! How would you settle these classic baseball arguments?

ROBERTO ALOMAR HAD THE BEST ARM OF ANY BLUE JAY ...

… because he could make impossible throws look totally natural and easy. Second basemen don't get to show off their throwing power often. However, when Alomar fielded balls near second base, his throws got to first like they were shot out of a cannon. There is a reason he won five Gold Gloves during his five years in Toronto—and it wasn't just because he could pick up grounders!

SPEAKING OF CANNONS, LET'S TALK ABOUT JESSE BARFIELD ...

… because when he had the ball in his hand, no runner even thought about advancing to the next base! Barfield (LEFT) played right field for the Blue Jays from 1981 to 1989. He threw out more than 100 runners during that time. Nothing was more fun than watching Barfield deliver a strike to home plate from 300 feet away—and seeing the look on a baserunner's face when he was out by a mile.

... because he could throw it for a strike anytime he wanted to. Halladay would wait until a batter was expecting a fastball and then drop his hard, sharp-breaking curve for a strike. Halladay's curve was so good that even if a hitter outguessed him and was waiting for the pitch, it still broke too sharply to hit.

DAVE STIEB FANS MIGHT WANT TO HAVE A WORD WITH YOU ...

... because he threw a curve that drove batters crazy. Stieb (RIGHT) was a small pitcher with a big fastball. He threw it inside to make opponents back away from home plate. When the moment was just right, Stieb would confuse a batter with a soft, slow curveball. The pitch looked like it had rolled off a table. Steib made a lot of very good hitters look very bad.

Toronto Blue Jays
pitcher DAVE STIEB lanceur
Card Number 22 of 24 - Carte Numéro 22 de 24
© 1981 O-Pee-Chee Co. Ltd. Printed in Canada - Imprimé au Canada

The great Blue Jays teams and players have left their marks on the record books. These are the "best of the best" …

Paul Molitor

BLUE JAYS AWARD WINNERS

WINNER	AWARD	YEAR
Alfredo Griffin	co-Rookie of the Year*	1979
Bobby Cox	Manager of the Year	1985
George Bell	Most Valuable Player	1987
Pat Borders	World Series MVP	1992
Paul Molitor	World Series MVP	1993
Pat Hentgen	Cy Young Award	1996
Roger Clemens	Cy Young Award	1997
Roger Clemens	Cy Young Award	1998
Eric Hinske	Rookie of the Year	2002
Roy Halladay	Cy Young Award	2003

The annual award given to each league's best first-year player.

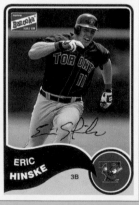

Eric Hinske

Roy Halladay

BLUE JAYS ACHIEVEMENTS

ACHIEVEMENT	YEAR
AL East Champions	1985
AL East Champions	1989
AL East Champions	1991
AL East Champions	1992
AL Pennant Winners	1992
World Series Champions	1992
AL East Champions	1993
AL Pennant Winners	1993
World Series Champions	1993

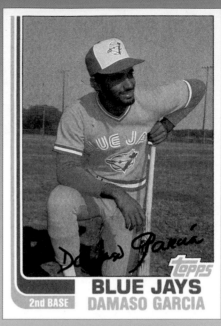

BLUE JAYS
DAMASO GARCIA
2nd BASE

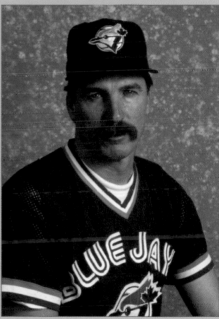

TOP: Damaso Garcia batted first in the lineup in 1985.
ABOVE: Jack Morris won 21 games in 1992.
LEFT: Dave Stewart went 12–8 in 1993.

PINPOINTS

The history of a baseball team is made up of many smaller stories. These stories take place all over the map—not just in the city a team calls "home." Match the pushpins on these maps to the **TEAM FACTS**, and you will begin to see the story of the Blue Jays unfold!

TEAM FACTS

1 Columbus, Ohio—*Pat Borders was born here.*

2 Atlanta, Georgia—*The Blue Jays won the 1992 World Series here.*

3 Tampa, Florida—*Fred McGriff was born here.*

4 Kansas City, Missouri—*Tom Henke was born here.*

5 Oklahoma City, Oklahoma—*Joe Carter was born here.*

6 Chicago, Illinois—*The Blue Jays won the 1993 pennant here.*

7 Saint Paul, Minnesota—*Dave Winfield was born here.*

8 Santa Ana, California—*Dave Stieb was born here.*

9 Seattle, Washington—*John Olerud was born here.*

10 Toronto, Ontario, Canada—*The Blue Jays have played here since 1977.*

11 Ponce, Puerto Rico—*Roberto Alomar was born here.*

12 San Pedro de Macoris, Dominican Republic—*Tony Fernandez was born here.*

Fred McGriff

AL EAST—A group of American League teams that play in the eastern part of the country.

ALL-STAR—A player who is selected to play in baseball's annual All-Star Game.

AMERICAN LEAGUE (AL)—One of baseball's two major leagues; the AL began play in 1901.

BULLPEN—The area where a team's relief pitchers warm up. This word also describes the group of relief pitchers in this area.

CANADIAN FOOTBALL LEAGUE (CFL)—The highest level of professional football in Canada. The CFL began play in 1958.

CY YOUNG AWARD— The award given each year to each league's best pitcher.

DISABLED LIST—A list of injured players who are not allowed to take the field.

EARNED RUN AVERAGE (ERA)—A statistic that measures how many runs a pitcher gives up for every nine innings he pitches.

FUTURISTIC—Having a modern style or design.

GOLD GLOVE—The award given each year to baseball's best fielders.

GRAND SLAM—A home run with the bases loaded.

LOGO—A symbol or design that represents a company or team.

MAJOR LEAGUE BASEBALL—The top level of professional baseball. The AL and NL make up today's major leagues. Sometimes called the big leagues.

MINORS—The many professional leagues that help develop players for the major leagues.

MOST VALUABLE PLAYER (MVP)— The award given each year to each league's top player; an MVP is also selected for the World Series and the All-Star Game.

NATIONAL LEAGUE (NL)—The older of the two major leagues; the NL began play in 1876.

PASSION—Intense emotion.

PENNANT—A league championship. The term comes from the triangular flag awarded to each season's champion, beginning in the 1870s.

PLAYOFFS—The games played after the regular season to determine which teams will advance to the World Series.

REPETITION—The process of repeating something again and again.

RESOURCEFUL—Able to find quick and clever solutions to problems.

RETRACTABLE—Able to be pulled back.

ROOKIE—A player in his first season.

STARTING ROTATION—The group of pitchers who take turns beginning games for their team.

VETERANS—Players who have great experience.

WORLD SERIES—The world championship series played between the American League and National League pennant winners.

EXTRA INNINGS

TEAM SPIRIT introduces a great way to stay up to date with your team! Visit our **EXTRA INNINGS** link and get connected to the latest and greatest updates. **EXTRA INNINGS** serves as a young reader's ticket to an exclusive web page—with more stories, fun facts, team records, and photos of the Blue Jays. Content is updated during and after each season. The **EXTRA INNINGS** feature also enables readers to send comments and letters to the author! Log onto:

www.norwoodhousepress.com/library.aspx

and click on the tab: **TEAM SPIRIT** to access **EXTRA INNINGS**.

Read all the books in the series to learn more about professional sports. For a complete listing of the baseball, basketball, football, and hockey teams in the **TEAM SPIRIT** series, visit our website at:

www.norwoodhousepress.com/library.aspx

ON THE ROAD

TORONTO BLUE JAYS
1 Blue Jays Way
Toronto, Ontario, Canada M5V 1J1
(416) 341-1000
toronto.bluejays.mlb.com

NATIONAL BASEBALL
HALL OF FAME AND MUSEUM
25 Main Street
Cooperstown, New York 13326
(888) 425-5633
www.baseballhalloffame.org

ON THE BOOKSHELF

To learn more about the sport of baseball, look for these books at your library or bookstore:

• Augustyn, Adam (editor). *The Britannica Guide to Baseball*. New York, NY: Rosen Publishing, 2011.

• Dreier, David. *Baseball: How It Works*. North Mankato, MN: Capstone Press, 2010.

• Stewart, Mark. *Ultimate 10: Baseball*. New York, NY: Gareth Stevens Publishing, 2009.

INDEX

PAGE NUMBERS IN **BOLD** REFER TO ILLUSTRATIONS.

Alomar, Roberto 9, 16, **17**, 22, **22**, 40, 45

Arencibia, J.P. 10, 36

Ault, Doug 36

Bailor, Bob 6

Barfield, Jesse 7, 20, 34, 40, **40**

Bautista, Jose 10, 11, **11**, 23, 28, **28**, 35, 37, 39

Bell, George **6**, 7, 20, 26, 34, 37, **37**, 42

Boddicker, Mike 27

Borders, Pat 18, **18**, 42, 45

Burnett, A.J. 10

Carter, Joe 9, **9**, 16, 19, **19**, 22, 39, 45

Cecil, Brett 10

Cerone, Rick 6

Clemens, Roger 9, 42

Cone, David 9, 17

Cox, Bobby 24, 42

Delgado, Carlos 9, 22, 35, **35**, 38, **38**

Dixon, Ken 26

Ducey, Rob 27

Escobar, Yunel **4**, 10

Fairly, Ron 6, 34, **34**

Felix, Junior 31

Fernandez, Tony 7, 16, 21, **21**, 34, **34**, 45

Garcia, Damaso **43**

Garvin, Jerry 29

Gaston, Cito 24, 25, **25**

Green, Shawn 9

Griffin, Alfredo 7, 42

Guzman, Juan 17, 19, **34**

Halladay, Roy 10, **10**, 23, 35, **35**, 38, 41, 42, **42**

Henderson, Rickey 16, 19

Henke, Tom 17, 21, 45

Hentgen, Pat 9, 17, **35**, 42

Hill, Glenallen 29

Hinske, Eric 42, **42**

Howell, Roy 6

Key, Jimmy 7, **7**, 17, 21

Lilly, Ted 10

Lind, Adam 10, **14**

Maldonado, Candy 17

Mayberry, John 6

McGriff, Fred 7, 27, **27**, 45, **45**

Molitor, Paul 9, 16, 19, 38, 42, **42**

Morris, Jack 9, 17, **43**

Moseby, Lloyd 7, 20, 26, **26**, 30, **30**, 31x

Mulliniks, Rance 26

Olerud, John 9, 16, 36, **36**, 45

Romero, Ricky 11, 37, 39, **39**

Schilling, Curt 19

Shields, James 36

Sprague, Ed 17

Staggs, Steve **15**

Stewart, Dave 9, 17, **43**

Stewart, Shannon 9

Stieb, Dave 7, **8**, 20, 41, **41**, 45

Thomas, Frank 35

Upshaw, Willie 7

Ward, Duane 17

Wells, David 9

Wells, Vernon 10, 23, **23**, **33**, 39

White, Devon 9, 16

Whitt, Ernie 26, 27, 31, **31**

Williams, Mitch 19

Winfield, Dave 9, 16, **16**, 18, 45

ABOUT THE AUTHOR

MARK STEWART has written more than 50 books on baseball and over 150 sports books for kids. He grew up in New York City during the 1960s rooting for the Yankees and Mets, and was lucky enough to meet players from both teams. Mark comes from a family of writers. His grandfather was Sunday Editor of *The New York Times,* and his mother was Articles Editor of *Ladies' Home Journal* and *McCall's.* Mark has profiled hundreds of athletes over the past 25 years. He has also written several books about his native New York and New Jersey, his home today. Mark is a graduate of Duke University, with a degree in history. He lives and works in a home overlooking Sandy Hook, New Jersey. You can contact Mark through the Norwood House Press website.